SUMMER OF 2020

SUMMER OF 2020

KYSMetrist

CITI OF
BOOKS

CITIOFBOOKS, INC.
3736 Eubank NE Suite A1
Albuquerque, NM 87111-3579
www. citiofbooks. com

Hotline: 1 (877) 389-2759
Fax: 1 (505) 930-7244

Ordering Information:
Quantity sales. Special discounts are available on quantity purchases by corporations, associations, and others. For details, contact the publisher at the address above.

Printed in the United States of America.

ISBN-13: Paperback 979-8-89391-193-0
eBook 979-8-89391-194-7

Library of Congress Control Number: 2024914496

PREFACE

I started this journey, sharing my work on my Facebook page Back to the Beginning, in the midst of the age of Oscar Grant, Sandra Blanc, Danny Ray Thomas, Eric Garner, Michael Brown, Trayvon Martin, Ahmaud Arbery, Breonna Taylor, and George Floyd, who screamed in his death, "Be silent no more". These lives are known because they made the headlines. There are many more lives that were horrifically ended but their stories have gone buried, double meaning intended.

June 2020, I began posting daily words that were inspired by my reading through the Bible, daily events, and personal reflections. Week 1 declared You **WOKE** up, Week 2 exclaimed, You are **AWAKE**... Week 3 is a reminder, You **ARE**... I asked the followers to return to see how the month on June concludes.

The final full of week June 2020 we examined ourselves. You have journeyed with me for 21 days, 6 days of daily postings followed by Sunday Sage, readings that are recorded and uploaded to soundcloud.com/karla-sutton-mckinney. June closes in Week 4, with **YOU.**

We have arrived at the end of June.

You have engaged with me for 29 days. Each of these days required that I sit and wait for God to give me words to convey His Word to you. What a journey. Around Day 8, I started to worry. Then I remembered, He told me what He wanted to do and what I needed to do, agree. It was in this agreement that June's Juxtaposition came to life.

July introduces Justice.

July is complete with talk of Justice. After all the events leading up to and through June, it is time for Justice to speak. Justice will be characterized in many ways. Justice will speak. Justice will listen. Justice will demand action. Then in the end, Justice will identify itself. Justice is Jesus. Justice will ask the Believers to look at their own lives and actions. Then after all is said and done, Believers will have to decide if they truly are on the side of JUSTICE.

August examines the events of March through June and the Justice that July personified. August will also directly reference, George Floyd, Justice Ruth Ginsburg and Civil Rights Activist and long-term Rep. for the 5th District, John Lewis to include the passing of my Cousin, Shawn Allan Randall. August is calling for us not to forget why we are here in this atmosphere of hate, active racism, and apathy. August concludes with a reflection on Black Lives Matter, REALLY, then to who?

Enjoy.

JUNE'S JUXTAPOSITIONS

Forced stillness demands that we be awakened and aware. We are strongly cautioned and pressed. We are called; actually, challenged to listen and attune our hearts with the hope of application.

Accountability and acceptance are presented as required to achieve the "necessary" thing. Why all of this? As receivers we must do something with what we have taken in; what we do with what we have understood defines us.

June's reflections call us to a place that demands more: focus, examination, persistence. Prepped and prepared; stay the course and make use of your privileged freedom.

Authored by

Karen D. Sutton, LCSW

Brighter Futures Now, LLC

June 1

Good Morning,

You WOKE up

Weigh your options.
Is the balance level?
What weight must you take.
What weight must you give.
To live

Reading Job 6:1

June 2

Good Morning,

You WOKE up
Recall the conversations
of yesterday,
Some download and save.
Others select to erase.

Reading Job 8-11

June 3

Good Morning,

You WOKE up.
Today began
as days before,
His Grace and Mercy
Opened the door.

Yet, yesterday is not today.
And, today, will not be tomorrow.
Lay hold to this truth
To ease your sorrow

Reading Job 12-14 Focus: 12:7-12

June 4

Good Morning,

You WOKE up
Accept the balance will never be leveled.
Accept the world will never be settled.

Accept there will always be those who have a need.
Accept there will always be those who survive on greed.
Accept where you are, amid these two extremes.

Reading: Job 15-18

June 5

Good Morning,

You WOKE up.
Moments like this
are years in the making.
Do not be fooled,
GOD is shaking.

ME, You, and everyone else,
Shaking us off, our picture-perfect shelf.

Complacent, silent Show Piece.
Satisfied with the sowing,
Surprised by what reaps?

Reading: Job 19-21

June 6

Good Morning,

You WOKE up
To God,
To Yourself.
Then, Everyone else.

Interesting,
You
Connect
the two.
Have you asked,
What am I to do?

Reading: Job 22-24

June 8

Good Morning,

You are AWAKE
Have you determined
what to give,
what to take.

CHANGE is here.
CHANGE has always been.
CHANGE today, is not designed to mend.
CHANGE today, is destined to rend,
You from Me
Us from Them
You must RESOLVE
Before Called to DEFEND

Reading: Job 29-31

June 9

Good Morning,

You are AWAKE
The Earth quakes.
Sifting, then Shifting.
Collapsing, then Lifting
Now are you listening.

The Earth did speak.
Creation did teach.
We ignored its' cry,
now havoc wreaks.

Nothing will compare,
on the day we are called to share,
our life on Earth,
and what we did, while there.

Reading: Job 32-34

June 10

Good Morning,

You are Awake.
Wisdom, awaits.
Understanding, seeks.
Knowledge, defeats.
Weigh the three
against Complacency.

And, if it reveals,
you are standing still,
yield to the truth,
Reset, then rebuild.

Reading: Psalm 35-37

June 11

Good Morning,

You are AWAKE
Accost your awareness
to your present state.

Lay open unfairness
to what it equates.

Confiscate today
By the Impact
You make.

Reading: Psalm 38-40:2

June 12

Good Morning,

You are AWAKE
What did the night conceal,
that the morning revealed?

That He is Great,
unsearchable are His ways,
understanding His existence
Man cannot explain,
Listen.

Today is happening,
with it you rose.
Did you ask for His guidance?
Because only He knows.

Reading: Psalm 40:3-42:17

June 13

Good Morning,

You are AWAKE
consciousness stirred,
vision unblurred,
SPEAK, unheard.

Reading: Psalm 1-9

June 15

Good Morning,

You ARE
Here... HEAR!
Conditions Clear?
Speak
Teach
Reach

June 16

Good Morning,

You ARE
Formed and Commissioned
Fashioned for Resistance
Framed to Maintain
Forgiveness in HIS name.

Focus averted?
YOU have been alerted

Reading: Psalm 21-25

June 17

Good Morning,

You ARE
Positioned to Execute
Postured for the Destitute
Poised from Perfection
Pardoned from your Misdirection.

Pathway undarkened?
to HIS voice will you harken?

Reading: Psalm 26-31

June 18

Good Morning,

You ARE
Conscious
With-in
With-out
TRUE Life
Cast out, All doubt.

About,
Our Truth
Our Lies
Our Birth
Our Demise
Engendering action
The WORLD belies

Reading: Psalm 32-35

June 19

Good Morning,

You ARE
Silent.
YET Provoked.
Compliant,
YET Choked.
Salient,
YET Dismissed.
Tired?
Then Resist

Happy JUNETEENTH

Reading: Job 36-39

June 20

Good Morning,

You ARE
Resolute,
NOW Render.
Soul,
NOW Tender.
For CHANGE.

Impact
Certified,
Reconcile
Or Collide.
Your ETERNITY rests
On what YOU Decide.
Celebrating Juneteenth

Reading: Psalm 40-44

June 22

Good Morning,

YOU
Still HERE!
Still STANDING!
Still MARCHING!
Still DEMANDING!

AND

Still destroying
Still defacing
Still dodging
Still debasing

ME
Still Teaching?
Still Preaching?
Still Praying?
Still Reaching?

OUR beginning AND end will one day meet.
Life in between - seeks our defeat.
See the horizon?
No longer obscure.
Question is
Can WE endure?

Reading: Psalm 51-56

June 23

Good Morning

"YOU
Valiant
Vigilant
Vindicated
Victor"
These are the words
OUR FATHER whispers.

"No need to run
No need to hide
If in ME
is where You abide."

"Frontline warrior?
Rear Attachment?
Placement vital,
suffer your combatant."
I know - YOU know
Victory is OURS
STANDFAST Soldiers
Don't you cower!

Reading: Psalm 57-62

June 24

Good Morning,
YOU,

Drink my Frustration
Dance on my Affliction
Dawdle with Reform
Deny with Derision

Frustrated no more
Afflicted with joy
Reformed within
Derision now, depends.

On how I see YOU
On how I see ME
Silenced only
If with YOU, I agree

Reading: Psalm 63-68

June 25

Good Morning
YOU,

Pardon my decision
To continue living.

In Spite of the hate
In Spite of the weight
In Spite of the attempts
of my being to erase.

Guilty, I am,
of speaking the TRUTH
Innocent, HE pronounced,
therefore, nothing to LOSE.

There is PEACE,
In what I have said.
Come from amongst
the LIVING DEAD.

Submit
Surrender
Salvation is OURS.
The greatest weight
Not knowing the day or hour

Reading: Psalm 69 – 72

June 26

Good Morning,

YOU
Consumer of All,
Consumer of Life.
Consumer of the Day?
Consumer of the Night?

Behold your dwelling place.
Evaluate the seller's bait.

Inventory the merchandise.
Consider now, your compromise.

Be wary,
Be wise.
Be hasty,
Foolishness cries.

Contend no more,
on the wavering road.
Witnesses declare,
The TRUTH you told.

June 27

Good Morning,

YOU tired?
I am!
This back and forth
Was not HIS plan.
Can you imagine
what this life would be?
If we kept our sight
on eternity.

Trouble was promised.
Protection, likewise.
Let US agree,
We, lose sight of our Guide.

HE has not moved.
HE will not change.
HE has refused,
to change the game.

June 29

We have arrived at the end of June.
You have engaged with me for 29 days. Each of these days required that I sit and wait on God to give me words to convey His Word through poetry.
What a journey.
Around Day 8, I started to worry.
Then I remembered what He told me He wanted to do and what I needed to do, was agree. It was in this agreement that June came to life.
If you have followed me from June 1, 2020, then this should sound familiar....

Good Morning,
You WOKE UP.
You are AWAKE.
YOU are.
YOU.

Return tomorrow for June's review.

June 30

Good Morning,
You WOKE up from a
Conscious Sleep [Sleepwalking]
You are AWAKE to
Covered Revelations [Denial]
You ARE
Convicted Liberators [Free]
You
Christ Captives [Seize]

Plainly spoken:
Stop Sleepwalking through life
Denying the obvious
We are Free
Seize

JULY'S JUSTICE

We witnessed the senseless loss of life by a system that is called to "protect and serve". However, what was meted out was unspeakable judgement by a jury void of humanity.

July was a month of clear vision for all the world to see into the realities of how to differentiate between God's Justice and man's justice.

Back-to-the Beginning's collection of July's Justice writings amplified the voice of God against the injustices and inhumane acts that left question marks in the hearts and minds of those asking where's God?

God is still on the Throne reigning and ruling from on high and looking low with a grief-stricken heart steeped in a Clarion-call for His Body of Believers to take its place and stance without compromise. Justice and Righteousness is the Kingdom Way.

The Body of Believers are absent from the frontlines, our voices are needed in the hollow of despair, and our inaction cries for action.

July's Justice may have come and gone with the collection of writings but what remains is for the Body of Believers to watch as well as pray.

Authored by

L. Elaine Sutton

Justice Beat Talk Show Creator

July 1

Justice defined,
Is Justice blind?
Consider today,
Then push rewind.

I am certain,
God has peeped our curtain.
Contrived of pride.
Stitched with hate.
Finished in blood.

Stunned by our fate?

Believers and Unbelievers,
Many stand together, behind these
Master Weavers.

Curtain frayed?
True Worshipers prayed!
HE is coming back.
Is the Word of the Day.

Reading: Psalm 92-100

July 2

Justice Reigns,
from on high.
Justice Calls,
from deep inside.

The high, the deep,
are set to meet.
Encounters reveal,
one's deplete.

Of reason.
Of ration.
Of care.
Of compassion.
Steep imposition
Informs the taxing.

From the high?
From the deep?
Mute the chatter,
Your living SPEAKS.

Reading: Psalm 101-103

July 3

Justice Invades,
our bone and marrow.
Justice Ignites,
our joy and sorrow.

Justice Implodes,
our selfish ways
Justice Indicts,
for better days.

Reading: Psalm 104-105

July 4

Justice Exists,
For Me and You.
Justice Exposes,
Hidden truth.

Justice Examines,
The heart of man.
Justice Extracts,
What hatred demands.

Reading: Psalm 106-107

July 6

Justice does not cower
Under the peril of man's power.
Justice does not fade,
Under our protests and parades.

Justice does not negotiate
With our agreements and debates.
Justice does not cater
To our flesh, which we favor.

Justice will outlast,
our today and tomorrow
Justice will recompense
Our joy and sorrow

Justice will defend
Our life and death
Justice will judge
Every man's, last breath.

Reading: Psalm 113-118

July 7

Justice afflicts me,
in ways for my good.
Justice understands me,
in ways I am misunderstood.

Justice calls me,
in ways, I will perceive.
Justice upholds me,
Because I believe.

Reading: Psalm 119:1-72

July 8

We All wonder,
does Justice see
my plight?
Does Justice see
the young mothers in the night?
Does Justice see
the young fathers, fighting the good fight?
Justice declares,
"I stand to bare, the beauty in the blight."

Justice ask, "Would you stay awhile,
Remove the crowd
I AM that I AM
is speaking now.

Reading: Psalm 119:73-176

July 9

Justice does not Echo
It is the Voice
Justice is Living
BELIEVERS have no Choice.

Reading: Psalm 120-129

July 10

Justice rises,
to a world divided,
by Race and Religion
and Populace decisions.

Undecided in their truth,
Justice makes that Commute,
between dishonesty and equity,
pleading, "Where is verity?"

The plea will never change.
Yet we remain the same.
Protest what is plain,
Justice is Gain.

Reading: Psalm 130-136

July 11

Justice's depths
take my breath.
Uprooting the extremes,
Sowing my dreams.
Reminding me,
it is not what it seems.

So, if I say
"Justice fades!",
Where is my faith,
In this implication made.

Is it not the substance of my hope?
Is it not evidence in the unseen?
Is it not faith in what Justice means?

Reading: Psalm 137-143

July 13

Justice is not a spectator,
to the Believer,
Justice is a dictator.

Of Ways and Means
But you have absconded your seat
For life's finer things.

Redemption approaches.
Justice knows this.
The question is,
will your Vote show this?

Reading: Proverbs 1-3

July 14

Justice DID NOT stain the
Pavement.
Justice DID make a
Statement.

"In Me, you
Laid
In Me, you
Prayed

In Me, you
Clave
In Me, you
Gave
Your Life."

Justice saw.
The World sees.
Justice states,
"YOU Breathe."

Reading: Proverbs 4-6

July 15

The native,
Injustice
thrives
among us.
Man contrived,
petri fungus.

Uproot
the intruder.
Decry the node.
En graft the culture
with Love,
the Justice Code.

Reading: Proverbs 7-9

July 16

Justice INHABITS the earth.
The Righteous understand its' true worth.
Rejoicing together in endless mirth.
Justice tells, of OUR Rebirth.

It was written before time was to be.
Written to include, OUR eternity.
So, WE live OUR lives, to one day see,
Justice defend, OUR Not Guilty plea.

So, release the wicked,
do not mind their business
'every knee shall bow',
remember this?

Justice INHABITS the earth.
Pray and Watch
then Get to work!!!

Reading: Proverbs 10-11
Referencing: Philippians 2:10; Nehemiah 4:9

July 17

Justice lead me home.
Justice forbids me to roam.

Where the wicked gather
For their folly and laughter
Ignorant of today
and life hereafter.

Justice release me.
Justice Unleash me!
With calm or fury,
Justice, just hurry.

Reading: Proverbs 12-14

July 18

Justice,
weighs the balance,
supports of truth,
opposed of malice.
Unbalanced scales,
Tell.
Equilibrium
Hides.
Objective exposed,
You decide.

Reading: Proverbs 15-16

July 20

Justice is a Truth,
Not Conceived by Man.
Justice is a Truth,
That Ordered this Land.
Justice is a Truth,
That the Righteous Understand.
Justice is a Truth,
That is Lived as Contraband.

Reading: Proverbs 20-22

July 21

Political Speak...

Justice will not cater
Neither will Ruth Bader

Later,
Justice Ginsburg
As we will remember

Elevated our stature
Argued our factors
Refused to pander
Because Women matter

Obama Care faired
With her partial consent.
Trump prevailed
Amid her public dissent.

Justice engenders,
A worthy defender.
Justice Ginsburg,
Opinions tendered.

Reading: Proverb 23-24

July 22

Justice appreciates men of low esteem.
Justice depreciates men of great means.

Justice's contentions,
excused the lynching's,
Not to mention,
the Raping of women.

Not only Us
But Them as Well
Justice lingers to bid farewell.

To Saints who look away
To Sinners already displaced

You see…
Justice courts,
We continue to abort,
The Truth unblemished.
Reconcile before,
"It is finished."

Reading: Proverbs 25-28

July 23

What do we gain,
when Justice is restrained?
Perverted profit,
and all that is profane.

Examine the history.
No longer a mystery
Maybe your comfort.
Results of my misery?

It will not matter
how slight the offense,
Confession and Repentance
are our only defense.

Yet we worship divided,
knowing all we are provided,
refusing this Truth,
Justice is not Undecided.

Reading: Proverbs 29-31

July 24

Justice laments
Separate but Equal
Shards of that ruling
Have written the sequel
That we live today.

Coded talk
Dishonest walks,
Secretion of,
Unrighteous thoughts
What will restore,
the Separate but Equal,
American Folklore?

It will be,
ME and YOU.
Surrendering to,
The vanities of Life,
recalled Lot's Wife?

Justice laments,
Believers resent,
Separate but Equal
Justice's Advent.

Reading: Ecclesiastes 1-4

July 25

Justice,
My eyes are open.
My heart is broken.
No longer will I be a token,
Of
Success that is subjective.
Accomplishments that are rejected.
Gifts and Talents that are re-directed.

I AM
Fire tested
Purposely selected
Known to ONE
Of whom
I AM
wholly accepted.

Justice laughs.
I finally grasp.
My worthiness is
Justice Unmasked.

.

Reading: Ecclesiastes 5-8

July 26

To conclude my reading of Ecclesiastes today...

Justice fears
God.
Justice keeps
His commandments.

Justice agitates
Openly.
Justice silences
Propagandist

Reading: Ecclesiastes 9-12

July 27

Good Morning,
I begin this week and the conclusion of July with a talk with Justice...
each day will be a prelude to tomorrow.

"Part 1 of 4"

Justice,
you are my ointment.
Expunging,
my pain
Eradicating,
my disappointment.
Lubricating,
my wounds of hate.
Tell me,
why are we cell mates?

Reading: Solomon 1-8

July 28

"Part 2 of 4"

Confinement has a way
Of humbling a man,
Of exposing the truth,
to what he believes,
to what he will do.

What directs your mind,
Will direct your time.
Sleeping with those,
Of like kind.

Consider it,
do not resist
there is another position,
I cannot dismiss.

Truth they pondered.
Time was squandered.
So, Israel wandered.
Conscripted to be laundered.

Reading: Isaiah 1-4

July 29

"Part 3 of 4"

Guilt justified?
Conviction falsified?
Nonetheless,
JUSTICE was notified.

I AM your law.
Innocent and convicted
I AM your truth.
Hung with the wicked.
I AM your defense.
I CANNOT lie
I AM your JUSTICE
Who am I?

Reading: Isaiah 5-8

July's Justice

July 30

"Part 4 of 4"

Justice is Jesus,
To those who believe.
Justice is Jesus,
To those who receive.

His Love versus Hate
His Mercy then Grace
His Truth versus Lies
His Command to DENY,
Self.

Reading: Isaiah 9-11

REFLECTIONS ON 2020 AUGUST ASSAYS

July 2020 and man's form of *Justice* for the disenfranchised has morphed into the August *Clarion Call* for action and recompense. A call for swift action now with no reasoned delays is what they say. Is it really a call for Civil Action or a call for swift Reflection? For Believers, we are called to reflect on our Covenant with the Ancient of Days. Yes, that life-changing Covenant in which we promised to listen for His voice which may be saying "wait" for my instructions, for my lead. Scriptures says… *My sheep know my voice.* In this time of reflection do we hear/feel the urgency of the Call? Do we hear the admonishment to be standard-bearers, breach repairers, joy-givers where despair abounds? August prevails with us against digressing from Truth and to proclaim allegiance to the Covenant Relationship.

August calls us to acknowledge our conflictions, yet bids us to stand tall in our convictions. August reminds us to forfeit the blame and threat game and in whose hands judgment lies. Shocked, though we may be, at the burden we are asked to continue to bear, self-examination and repentance is still the order of the day. August says slow down and be keenly aware of the enemy and the many losses due to lack of wisdom. August reveals there are cracks in our armor and beseeches us to return to Hope and reclaim our stolen Praise.

But wait, all is not lost, there is still *good trouble* in which we can engage. We can/must proclaim our right to life, liberty, and pursuit of our destiny. This is what the Creator ordained and surely He will keep His promises. *Good trouble* takes a stand against captivity, denigration, and annihilation. It recognizes the fight is not against Race but the hardened hearts of Man. Thus, believers, we must be living witnesses. We are reminded of our commission to send out a full-throated *Clarion Call* even to deaf ears or be found hanging betwixt Life or Death.

August closes with the awful TRUTH that while some lives did not matter to OTHERS neither did they to US and so we must acknowledge our own self-loathing. We cannot not ignore the blood at OUR door. August ruefully proclaims that we (US and THEM) will answer for failing to adhere to the real Call—the Call to Christ and His transforming power.

Authored by
Ruby N. Gill

Mother

August Assays

<u>August 1</u>

No Poem, No Prose.
August Assays...
Juxtaposition's Justice is Jesus.
Think on this.
Believers.

Reading: Isaiah 18-22

August Assays

August 3

August settles in,
as July comes to an end.

August, what is on your mind?
"What will I do with the rest of my time?

June awakened me.
July hastens me,

'Confront your conflicting position,
or renounce your commission.'"

Reading: Isaiah 28-31

August Assays

August 4

August,
Complacency, what a horrid place.
What joy is there with the abased?

"You look on
and never within.
Easier that way
to dismiss your sin.

Call it
what you may,
Not gon' shield
with wordplay.

The tickling of the ears
is why we are here.
We continue to live
as if we have
nothing to fear.

Not from them
But from us."
Mmm,
Sincerely
August.

Reading: Isaiah 32-36

August Assays

August 5

August
do not fade.
Cast your shade,
for those betrayed
and underpaid,
the Enduring Fruit of
slave trade.
August, AUGUST
DO NOT fade.

Reading: Isaiah 37-40

Commentary -
The further away we get from life changing events, urgency needed then, seems to wane. I am getting settled here in Memphis, TN. Getting acquainted with the TFA chapter, they are involved and moving. I will not dismiss that this chapter and the alumni resemble more the demographics they serve. So, I conclude with this, something we have already heard, if not US then who?

Let us not forget...George Floyd, May 25, 2020

August Assays

<u>August 6</u>

August will measure,
the well of your treasure.

The wellness of your worship.
The profoundness of your praise.
The onus to obedience
toward a Covenant of ancient days.

Replete for replenishing?
Deplete toward diminishing?
Lower your vat,
sanctify your finishing.

August will measure,
the well of your treasure.
"…to will and to do
of his good pleasure."

Reading: Isaiah 41-43; Philippians 2:13

August Assays

August 7

August concedes,
Freedom rings.

Bell ringers are dying
Leaders are lying
Believers are nullifying
the Truth in His Word
by misapplying

Reproof and correction
for abject rejection.
Doctrine and instruction
for shameless seduction.

Freedom rings,
truth is revealed.
Freedom silenced,
truth is concealed.
Believers, Un-believers
Truth is in full swing.
August concedes
Freedom rings.

Reading: Isaiah 44-47

August Assays

August 8

August smolders,
with Louisiana's
Supreme stakeholders.

Maliciously they inflame,
to uphold a sentence,
so insane.

Bryant never denies
what the court proclaims.
"Harsh and excessive"
is his counterclaim.

With ancient Pig laws,
August smolders,
for the modern day
proud, Slave Owner.

Reading: Isaiah 48-51

August Assays

August 10

We are not all called to the same grind.
We are all called to have the same mind.

To have the mind of Christ...is...
to have the mind of Life.
Where equity begins and
where we end all strife.

Have not expectations of walking in unity,
if Christ is not the center of our community.

He is the only Way
to bridge the gap,
to mend the strain,
of His truth, we must retain.

With me, do not agree,
I beseech you to read,
to know for thyself,
what you honestly believe.

Reading: Isaiah 58-61

August Assays

August 11

The Lord says, "Wait patiently,
Circumstances urge you anxiously.

In life
In death
In what you give
In what you have left."

So, where in me,
does patience
have opportunity to breath?

He says, "you lose to win,
you are provoked to give in,
you are oppressed to your best,
you are suppressed to express.

That patience is often obscured,
by what you have been called to endure."

Patience is relative
to the measure of your faith,
Remember, it is on the LORD
we patiently wait.

Reading: Isaiah 62-66

August Assays

August 12

Christ will have YOU
examine,
this truth desert,
love famine
that YOU call life.
Christ will have YOU
take His Word,
all that YOU have heard,
and find delight.
Christ will have YOU
sit at His feet,
true relief,
and be complete.
Christ will have YOU.
Come, just as YOU are.

Reading: Jeremiah 1-4:4

August Assays

August 13

I will applaud His choice.
Yet, I dare not, in her, rejoice.
Until I hear her voice,
and the Truth she hoist,
that Christ is our Redeemer,
Living proof of a
Paid Invoice.

(Kamala Harris Nomination)

Reading: Jeremiah 4:5 – 6

August Assays

August 14

Believers, we live
our life full of error.
Believers, we are
accountable for mindless terror.
Believers, we are
to be the standard-bearers.
Believers, we are
to be breach repairers.
Believers, we are
to be joy for despair(er)s.
Believers, we are
to be color bearers.
Believers, we are
to be a sweet smelling savor.
Believers, we are
to be as Christ, our Savior.

Reading: Jeremiah 7-10

Commentary:
I do not know about you, but I need daily reminders of my life in Christ.

August Assays

August 15

My Memphis Moment....
I have come to this conclusion
Living has these intrusions
Life and Death,
Poverty and Wealth.
Where do you see yourself between the extremes?
To a Believer, this is what it means.
Life is defined by Death.
Poverty is the substance of our Wealth.
Christ came, reconciled these ends.
Believers, we must commit to contend,
with all that begs to widen the gap,
between those that have,
and those that lack.
Because in the end
when He redresses our sin,
He will say, "the intrusion was meant,
to welcome you in."

Reading: Jeremiah 11-14

August Assays

August 17

Jesus? Do you remember me?
I am the one you set free.
From myself, of course
My greatest enemy.

I have strayed from you
but just a degree,
yet after all these years
it looks like a hundred and eighty.

I am not okay.
I want to pray.
Words escape me
or maybe, I just do not know what to say.
Jesus said,
"Do YOU remember Me?"

Reading: Jeremiah 15-18

August Assays

<u>August 18</u>

When to agree
When to dissent
Consider the claim
Consider the intent

Truth cannot acquiesce
Truth is, we digress.
Truth is static, we are erratic
Truth is, to some, enigmatic.

The best we can do
is live equal with Truth.
Yet living beneath it,
is what we sometimes choose.

We plead, we bargain
with all manner of jargon,
with each act of defiance
our hearts are hardened;
to a Truth, to which
we refuse to hearken.

Agree or Dissent?
This is my claim,
the intent of which,
That you would call on
HIS name.

Reading: Jeremiah 23-25

August Assays

August 19

Ever been in this place,
This very, same, place,
when you want to run on
but God says, "wait".

You see from here,
to the next 20 years,
that path you are on,
God says, "is, just, too, clear.

You have not run upon,
not one stumbling block?
You add not a burden,
to the weight of your cross?

Is this road narrow?
Or is it wide?
Check your destination,
that prophet may have lied.

Ever been in this place,
this, very, same place,
Jeremiah came with a word,
that they chose to berate.

Reading: Jeremiah 26-28
Note: Causally related to my reading today.

August Assays

<u>August 20</u>

Why would I surrender
to the enemy's yoke?
Why would I dare
God to invoke,
His judgement,
His wrath,
His dismay,
His laugh?

Feeble at best
is my living,
then I cry to Him
because of His decision,
to have me report
for disobedience,
begging His court
for mercy and lenience.

From forever, has He spoken.
From forever, we have broken,
Covenant Relationship,
Faith and Trust,
then we dare ask why,
into the enemy's yoke,
we are thrust.

Reading: Jeremiah 29-31

August Assays

August 21

Have the Believers been following
the Democratic Convention?

King David was last
to get a mention?
Discern his heart,
and his intention,
less you grieve November,
for your inattention.

(Joe Biden accepting the Nomination)

Reading: Jeremiah 32 – 34

August Assays

<u>August 24</u>

My morning is quiet.
I resist being defiant.
Today is different.
No less significant.
To Them
To Us
To God,
in whom we trust.
So I surrender,
what I do not understand,
and trust His authority
at our last stand.
Knowing it flows
from His loving hand,
as we give up the Ghost,
at His command.

Be still the moment
of his passing.
Imagine this,
his collapsing,
into the arms
of His creator,
who then becomes
his respirator.
For life, for breath
without death,
for God knew

he had nothing left.
In that body
that was warn and tired.
Of his Father,
he had inquired,
of life everlasting
when his work
was done,
he secured his place
in his Father's Son.

While my morning
is quiet,
and I resist the urge
to be defiant.
I am calmed by the knowing,
that Shawn was compliant,
in answering his call
and completing
his assignment

To my cousin Shawn Allan Randall being laid to rest today.

Reading: Jeremiah 44-47

August Assays

<u>August 25</u>

My convictions
are weakened,
by my conflictions
of fight or flight;
shaped by the shadows
of black or white.

Which do I choose,
if with either, I lose,
my liberty or life
because I refuse,
to kowtow peacefully
to my grave;
but to stand uprightly
to cast my shade;
on hearts that so
proudly parade,
a hate that is
so utterly depraved.
To them, I say...

You commit this treason
of your malfeasance
upon my person
to which you have
sworn allegiance.

Yet, my convictions hold me,
while my conflictions scold me,
to demand my liberty and my life,
then I am reminded, of my Christ.

Reading: Jeremiah 48-49

August Assays

August 26

You cannot run,
you cannot hide,
so
do not smile,
do not snide,
the oppressed and oppressors are set collide.

Ancient History dictates,
God's Word mandates,
that a cleansing take place.

Therefore, let us not forget,
where judgement is first set,
holster your blame and ideal threats.

Examine your walk.
Examine your talk.
Examine your prayers.
Examine your thoughts.

What dream have you been chasing
while the retention of God, erasing?
Shocked at what we are facing?
Today resembles, fallen nations.

Yet, there is hope.
Repentance is in order.
Come to Him now,
less the brick and mortar.
We cannot run.
We cannot hide.
His Judgement is final
His will not be set aside.

Reading: Jeremiah 50-51.

August Assays

August 27

Let us slow down
Let us catch our breath
Let us take in
Both Life and Death.

To disregard either,
leaves the enemy
as the driver,
lost too many,
who were none the wiser.

Death has a knack,
of finding the cracks,
where time with Christ
has gone lacks.

And...

Events of these days,
have stolen our praise,
return to the HOPE,
that will never betray.

Life and Death,
to the Believer are ONE.
Complete in CHRIST,
the Resurrection.

Reading: Jeremiah 52 (Complete, tomorrow Lamentations)

August Assays

<u>August 28</u>

Good Trouble and I
have a date.
Good Trouble and I
cannot be late.
We did not orchestrate,
this inevitable convening.
We did agree to
no more quarantining.

Of our right to life,
Of our right to liberty,
Of our right to pursue,
our God ordained destiny.

It is what is granted
of our Creator.
It is what will be granted
of our legislators.

We Rise to March,
while many laments,
the raid on our person
with captivity, intent.

Captive to the point
of denigration.
Captive to the point
of annihilation.

Good Trouble and Us,
have come face to face.
With Truth that says,
"this is not about race."
Believers, we know this.
Yet, we choose to dismiss,
that the heart of man
needs a living witness.

Good Trouble and Us
have a date.
Good Trouble and US
cannot be late.
Good Trouble and Us
will not escape.
our inquisition
with Yahweh.

Reading: Lamentations 1-5

August Assays

<u>August 29</u>

Embrace your commission,
no matter who listens.
No matter who understands,
do not abandon His plans.

Consider your present.
Yesterday is departed.
Consider your future.
Abandon the halfhearted.

YES, abandon!!
or be held as ransom,
Paid in full,
by the world's cesspool.

Harsh this may be,
consider this imagery?
Life or Death,
choose your next breath.

Reading: Ezekiel 1-3 (The imagery here, is indescribable)

August Assays

August 31

It is the last day of August,
the Summer of 2020 magnified this...
Black Lives that did not matter
To THEM,
unfortunately, neither to US,
the truth must be spoken,
before we can honestly discuss,
our own self-loathing.

Who kills a man
for walking slowly across a street?
Who rejects a man,
because you say his words are incomplete?
Who refuses a man,
the right to an honest hustle?
Who provokes a man,
exasperated by his own struggles?

This list is endless.
These killings are senseless.
From THEM.
From US.
The truth must be spoken,
if we are to honestly discuss.
I cannot ignore,
the blood at my door,
or the day,
I will answer for...

the call, to cast a warning,
the call, to cease the mourning,
the call, to go adorning,
the call to Christ, and His transforming...
Power.

To Them...
From US...
Believers we are the ones who claim,
in "God we Trust."

You got it twisted.
You completely missed it.
Made real on the day,
you find you are blacklisted.

Once to live
Once to die.
Entry at His gate,
denied.

Black Lives did not matter
To Them
or
To US
the truth must be spoken
if we are to honestly discuss.

Reading: Ezekiel 8-11

ACKNOWLEDGEMENTS

"Let the words of my mouth, And the meditation of my heart, be acceptable in thy sight, O LORD, my strength, and my redeemer."

Ps. 19:14 KJV

All glory, honor, and praise belong to God, the Father, Jesus Christ, *my Lord and Savior,* and the Holy Spirit without whom these words would not have been possible.

Thank you!!!

Mom, Ruby Nell Davison, Sisters, L. Elaine Sutton and Karen D. Sutton for seeing value in this work and joining me in this endeavor.

Pops, Willie James Sutton and sister, Jaime "Jai" E. Sutton for the opportunity to persevere and endure toward abundance.

To my immediate family, husband of 27 years, Mark A. McKinney, sons, Kevin J. Pugh [Tomia], Christopher J. McKinney [Lana] and Anthony P. McKinney [Veronica] for opportunities granted to me by your lives, to learn, to grow, and to forgive.

To my extended families and friends in St. Louis, Missouri, Youngstown, Ohio, Atlanta, Georgia, Mobile, Alabama, surrounding areas and all places we were stationed as an active-duty *Army family,* for being a part of this journey because you are a part of **ME**.

To the Protestant Women of the Chapel (PWOC), where I began my journey sharing the Word of God, writing and sharing my poetry. *Hanau, Germany, 1998-2001.*

To the students at Westover High School in Fayetteville, North Carolina, in particular Daniel McKeller, Robert Boyd, Eric Bradley, Peter Robinson, and *Crystal Styles,* who gave me a glimpse into what my life's work would entail.

To the Staff, Teachers, and Parents at Westover High School, 2002-2008, I think on these days often. It was the beginning to my journey in education.

To the Staff, Teachers, Parents, and Students of DelaSalle Charter High School located in Kansas, Missouri, 2015-2020, you were my runway for today.

Blessings from ON HIGH, AMEN!!!